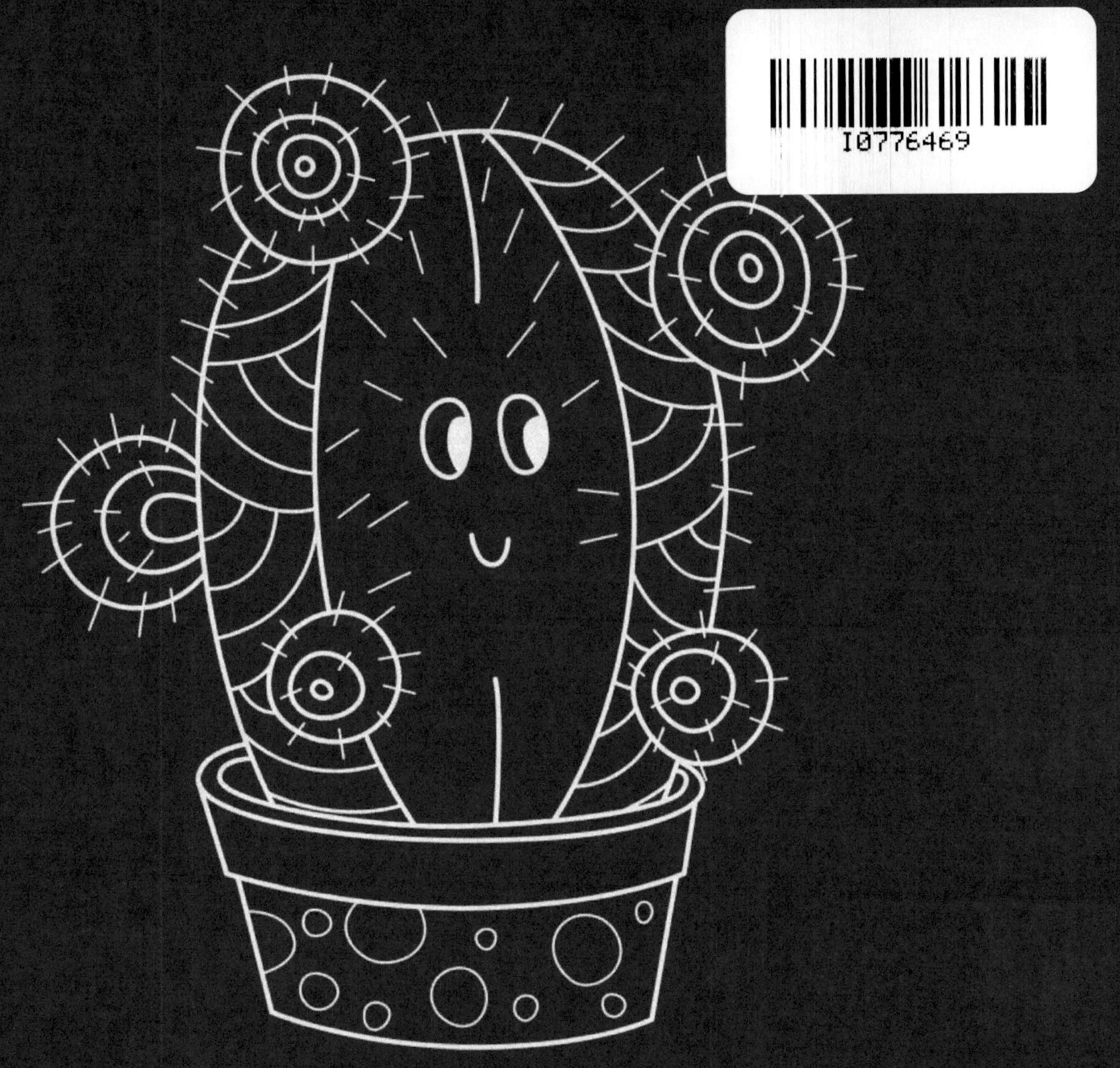

TINY CACTUS PUBLISHING

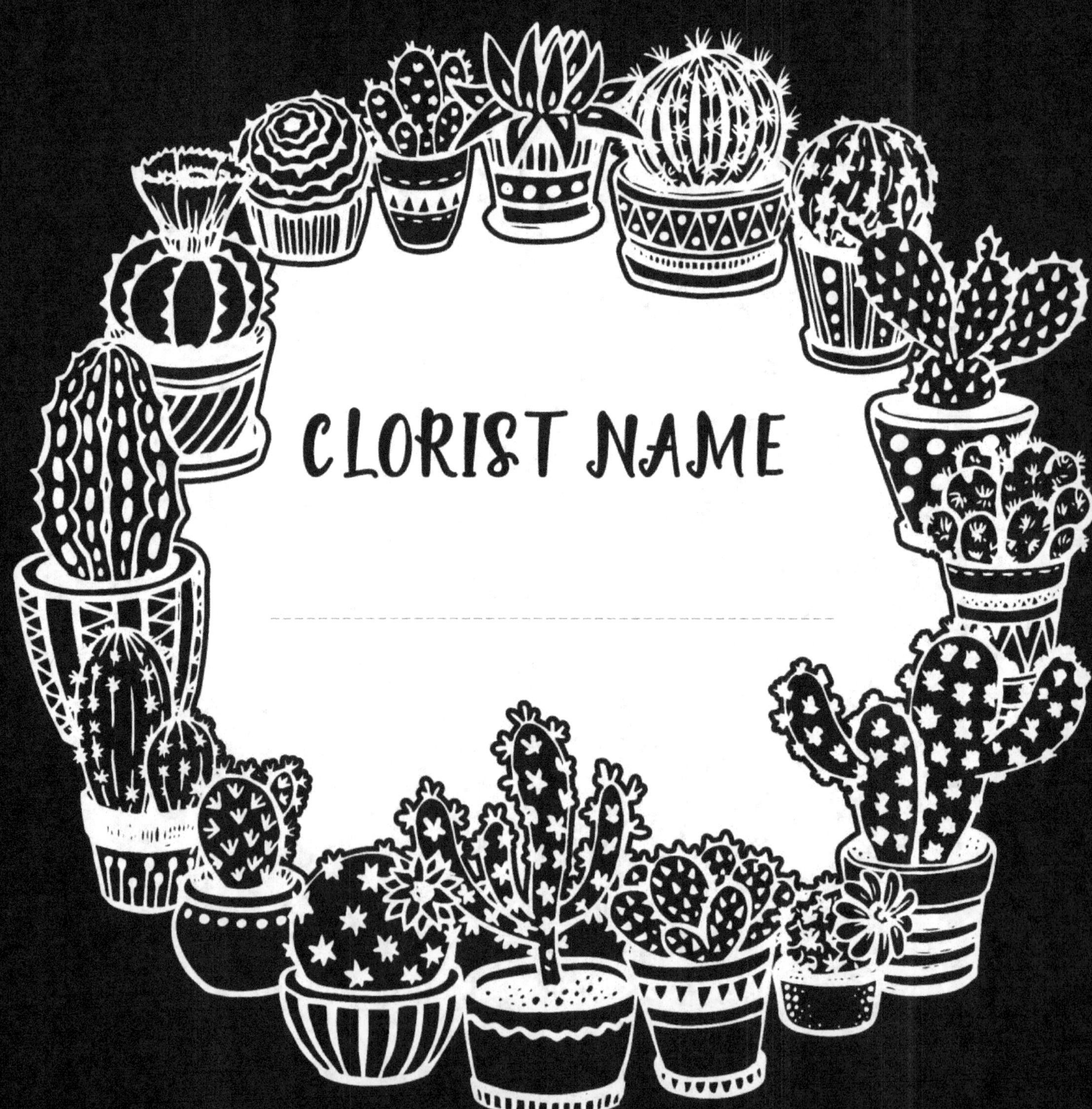

CLORIST NAME

TEST PAGE

PREPARE YOUR COLOR

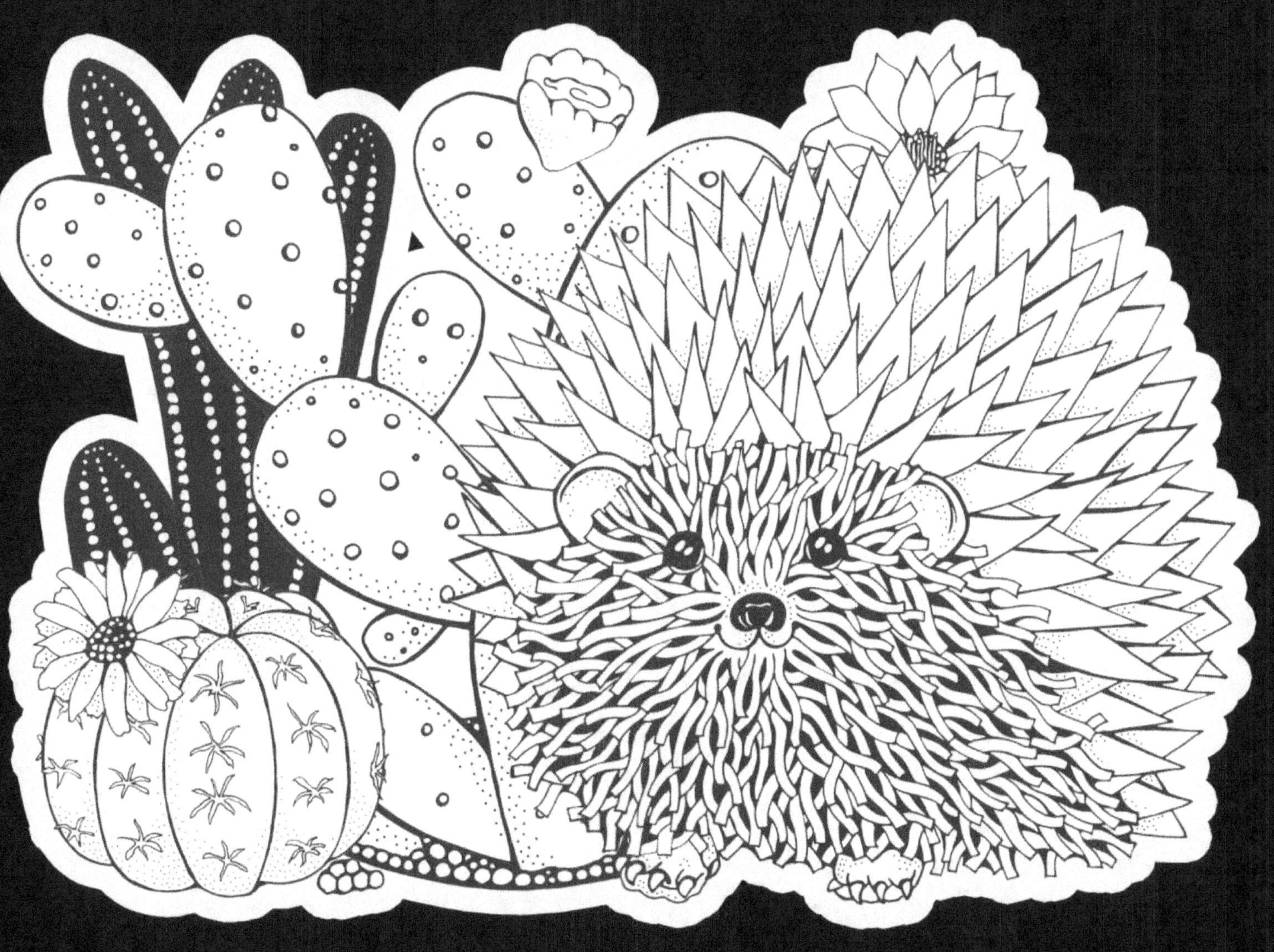

WARM UP !!

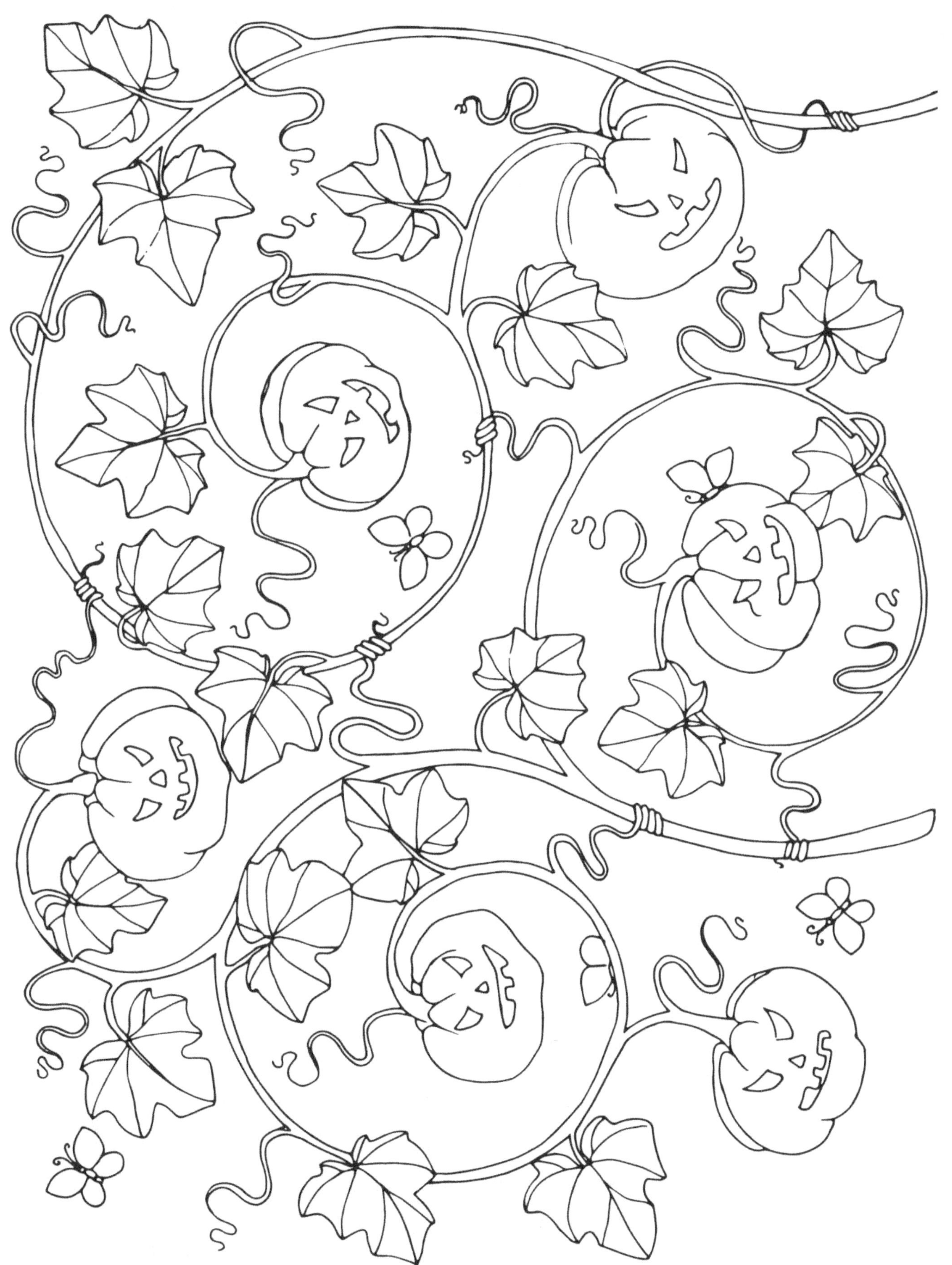

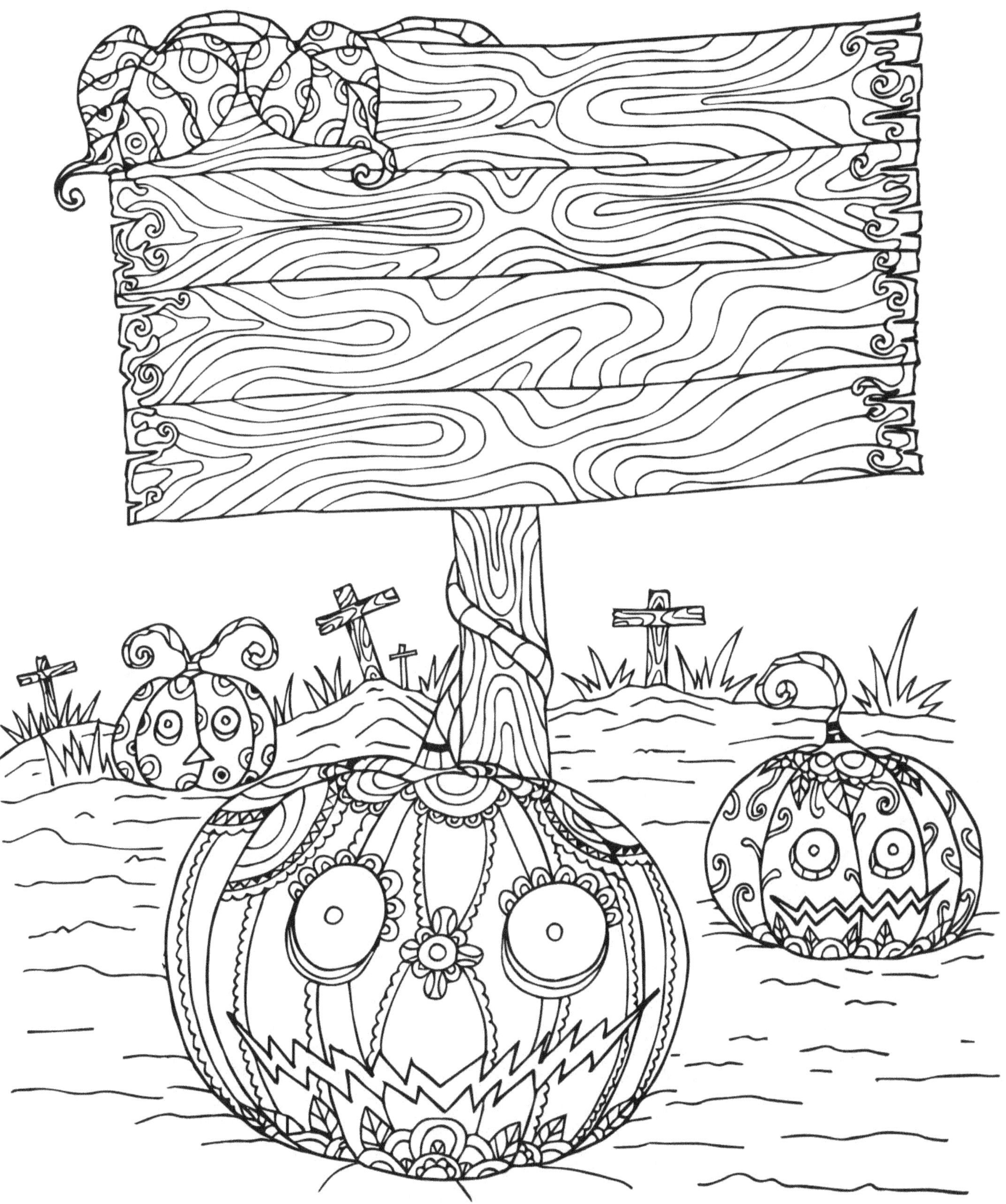

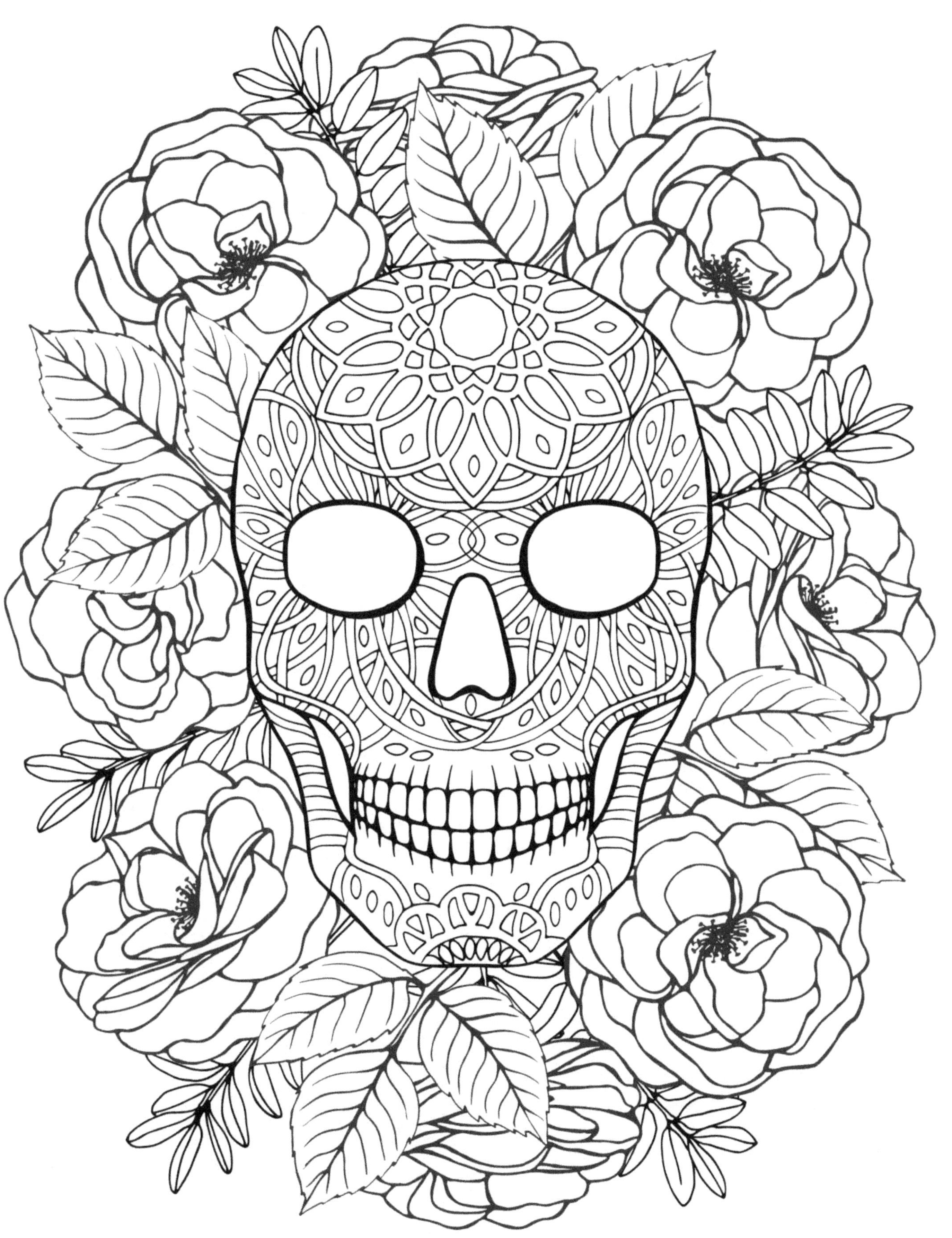

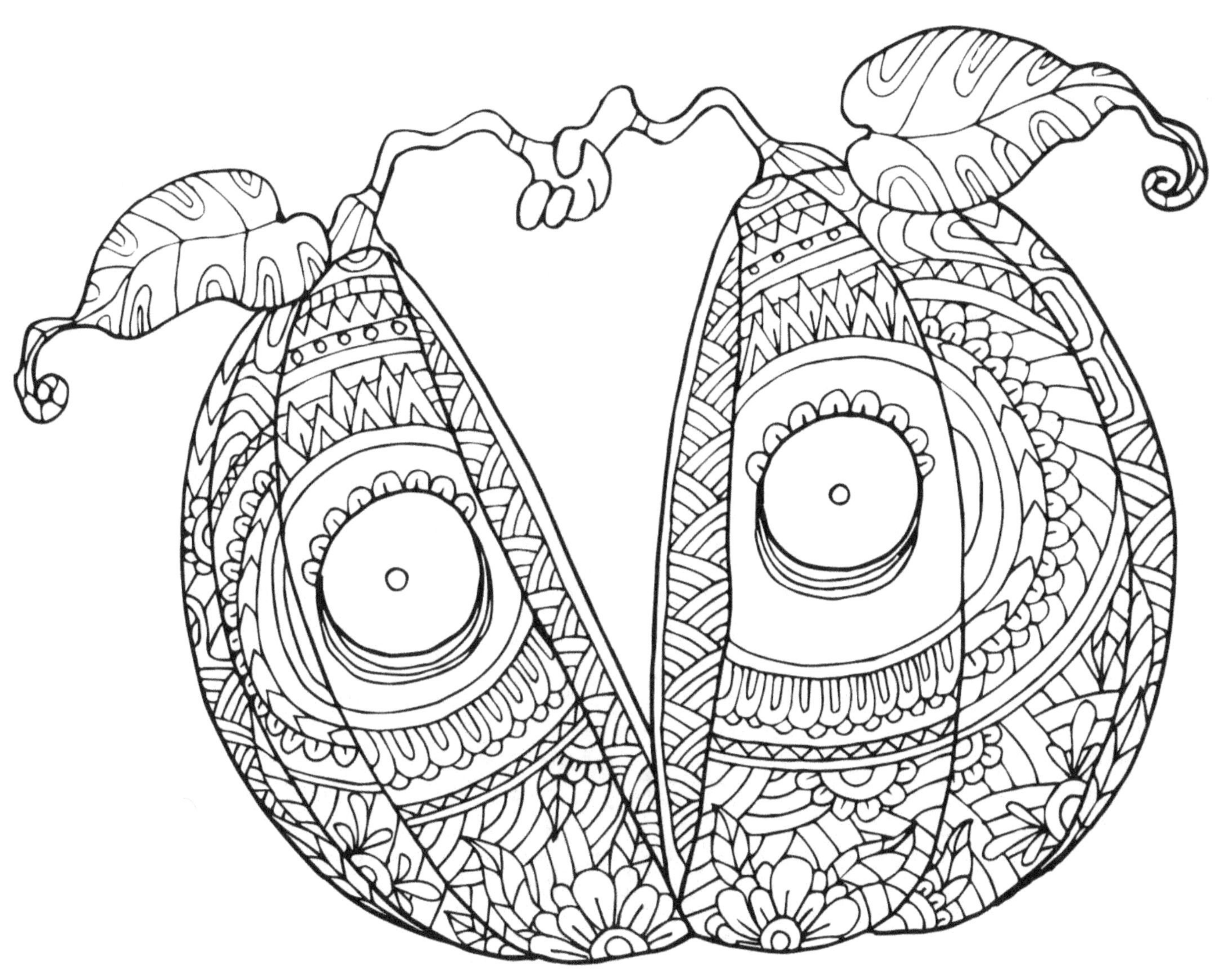

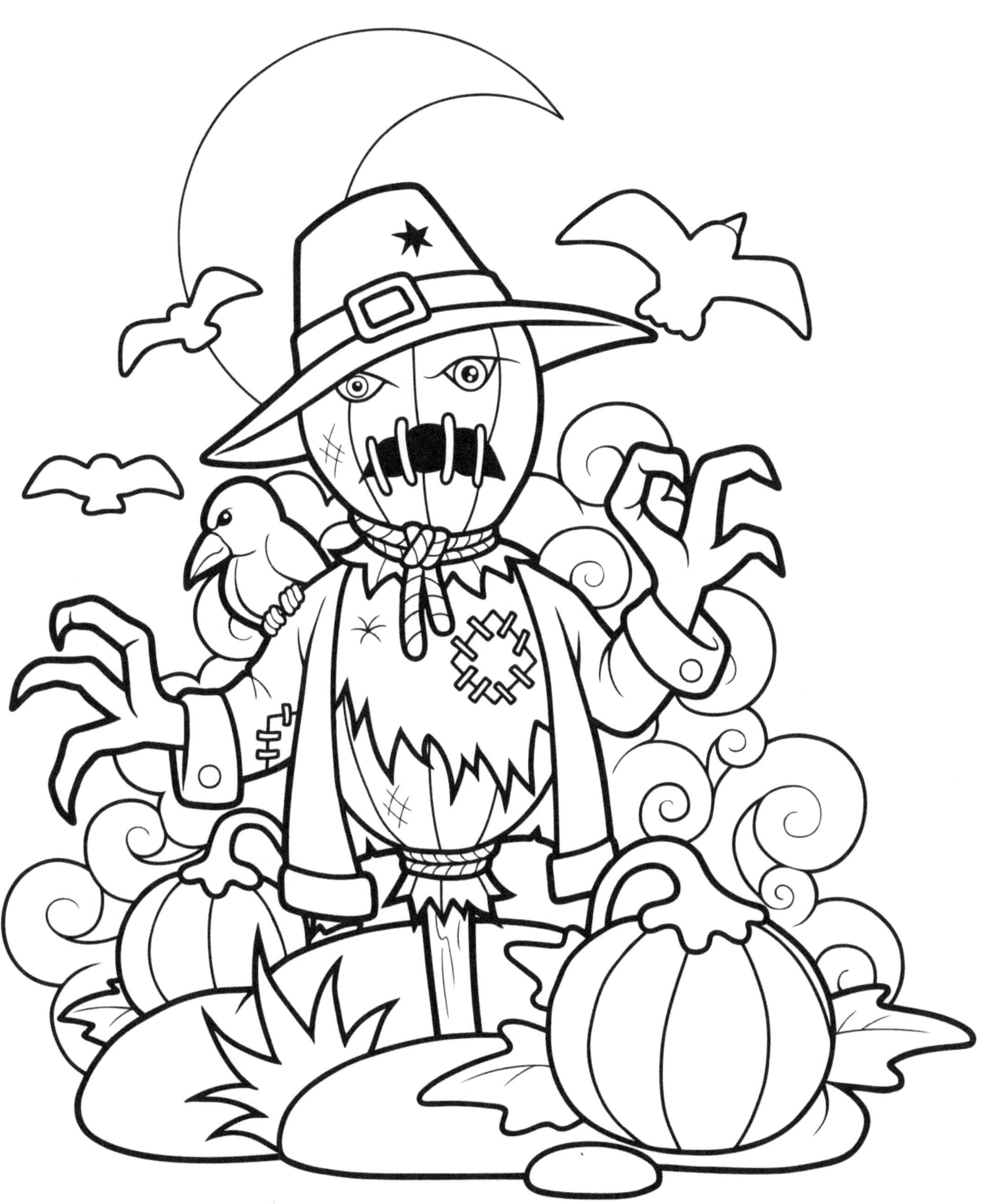

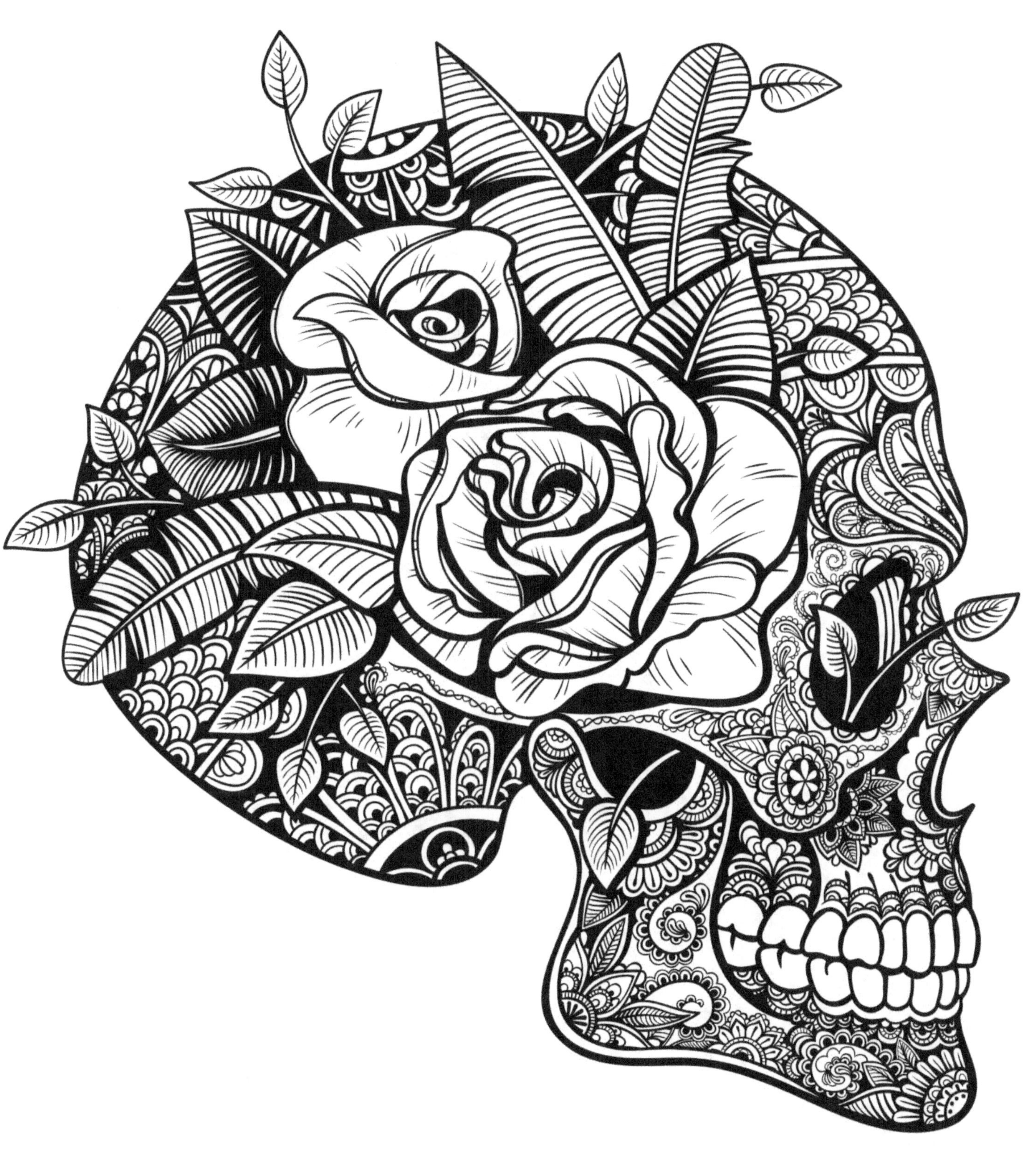

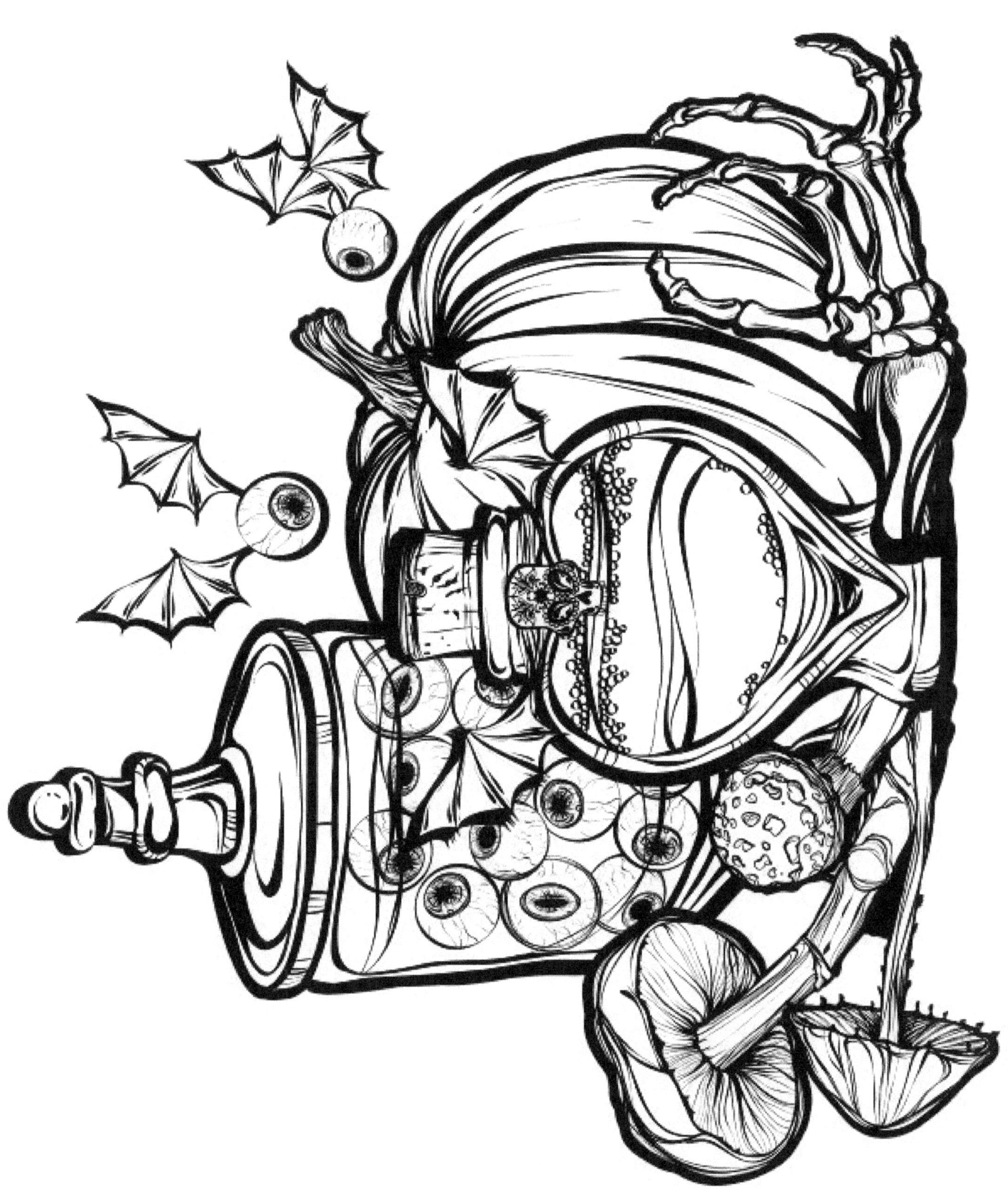

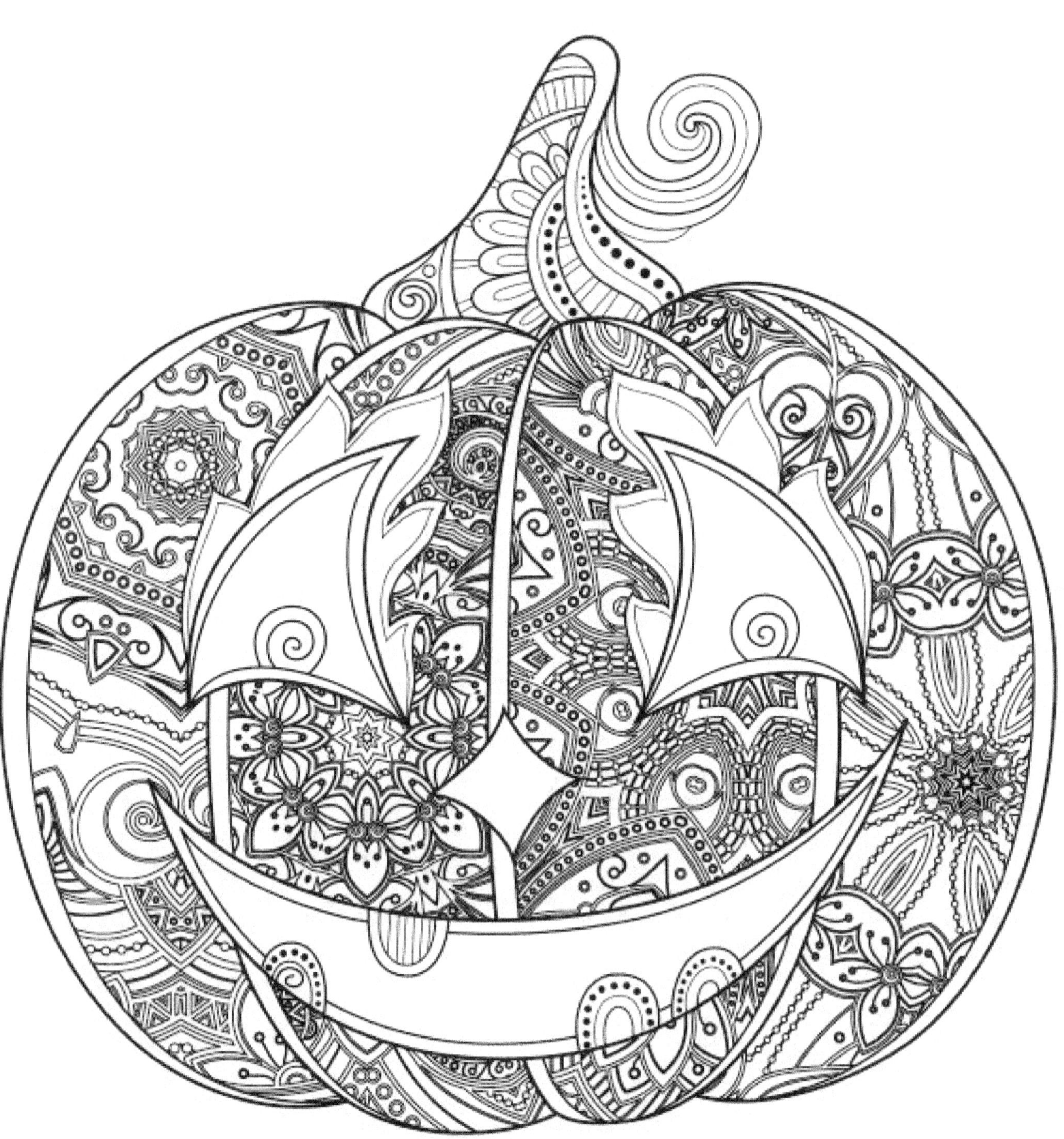

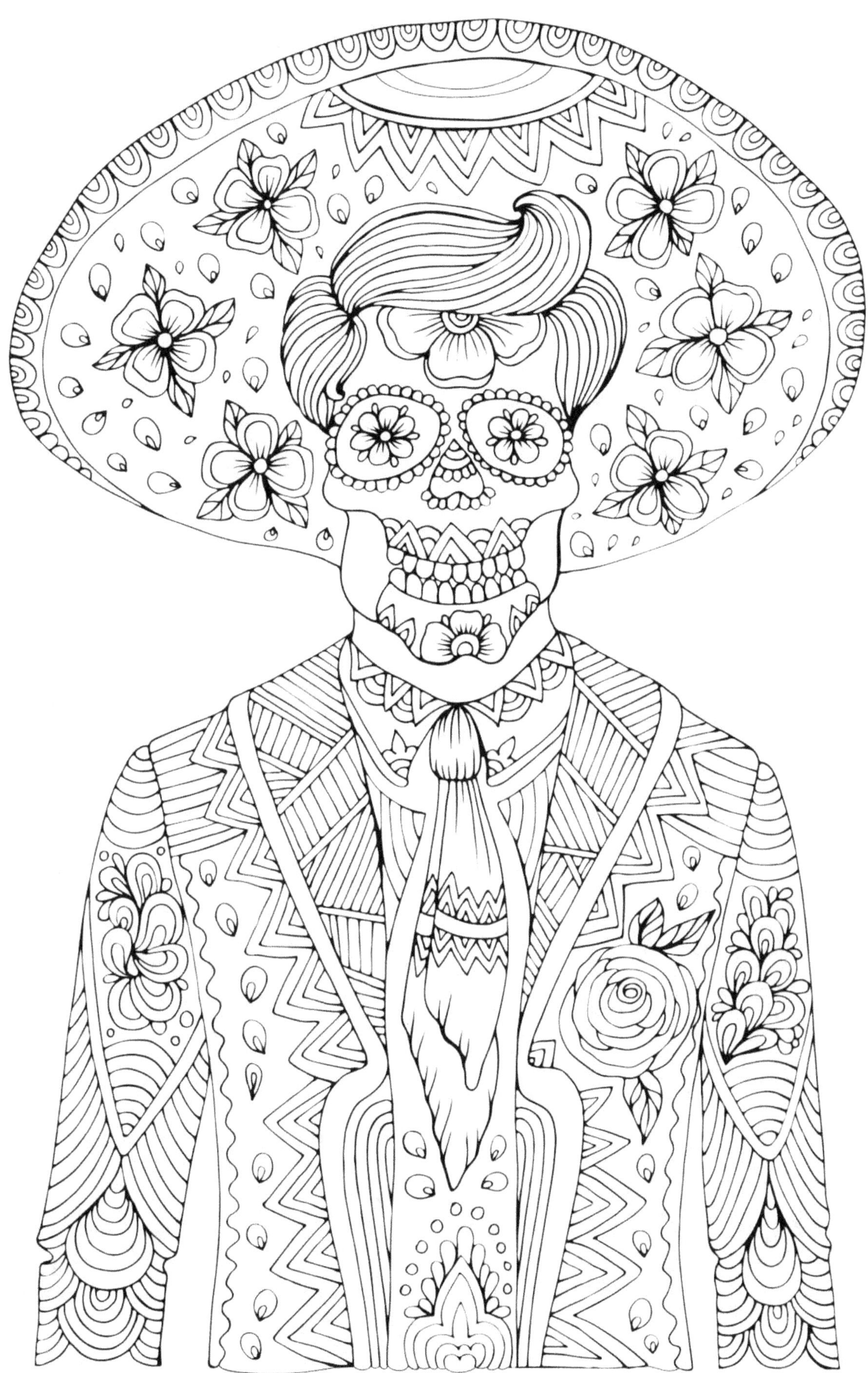

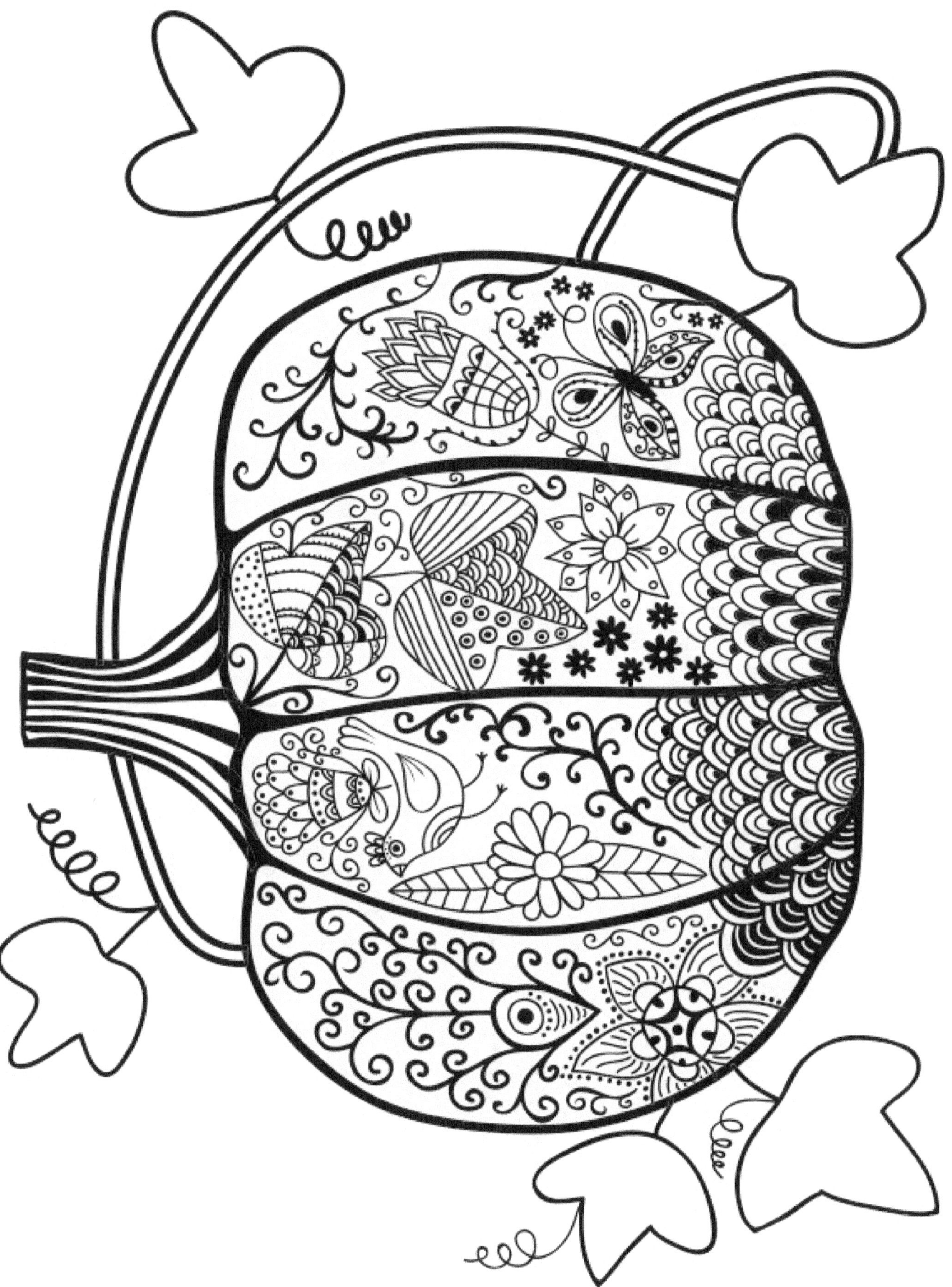

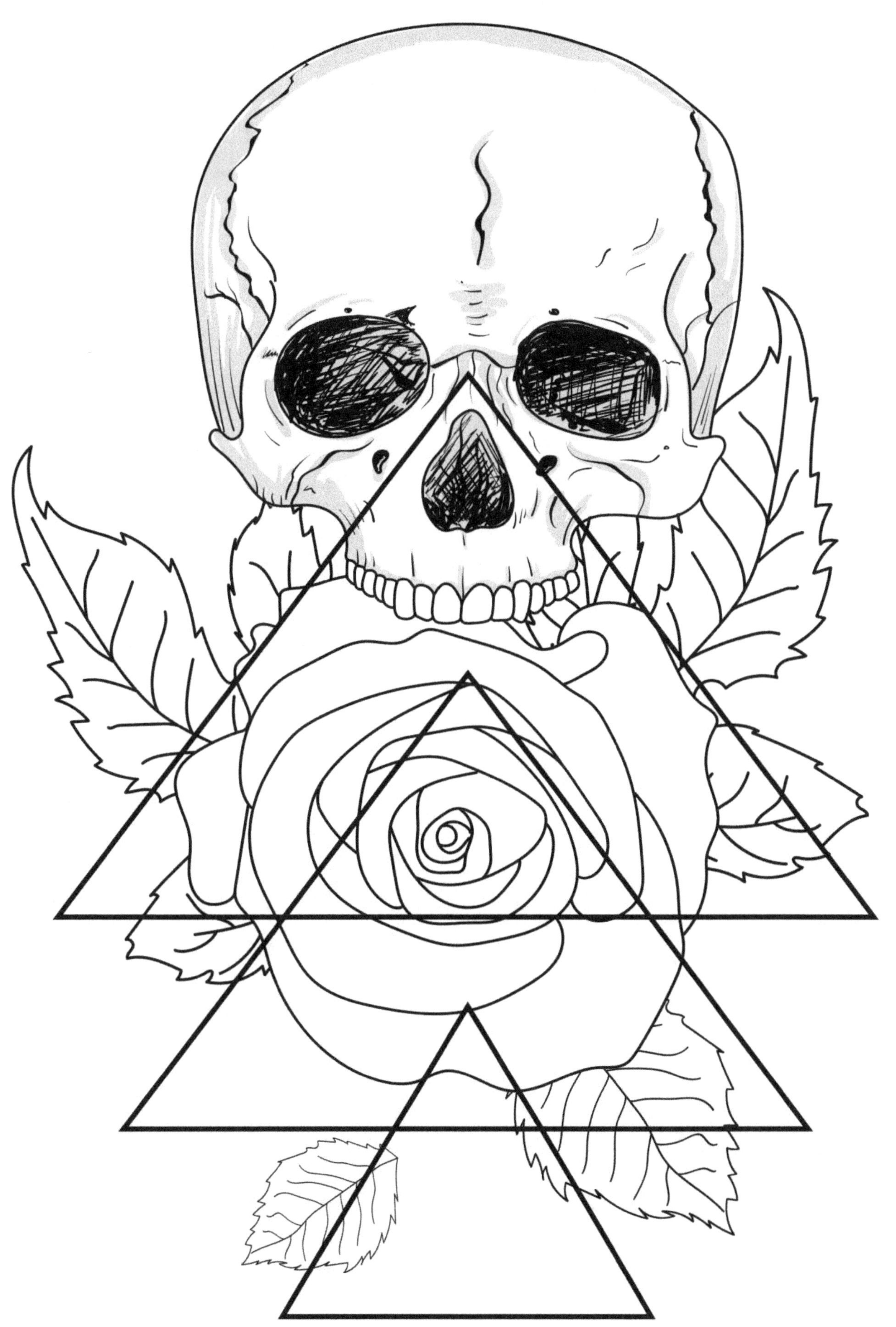

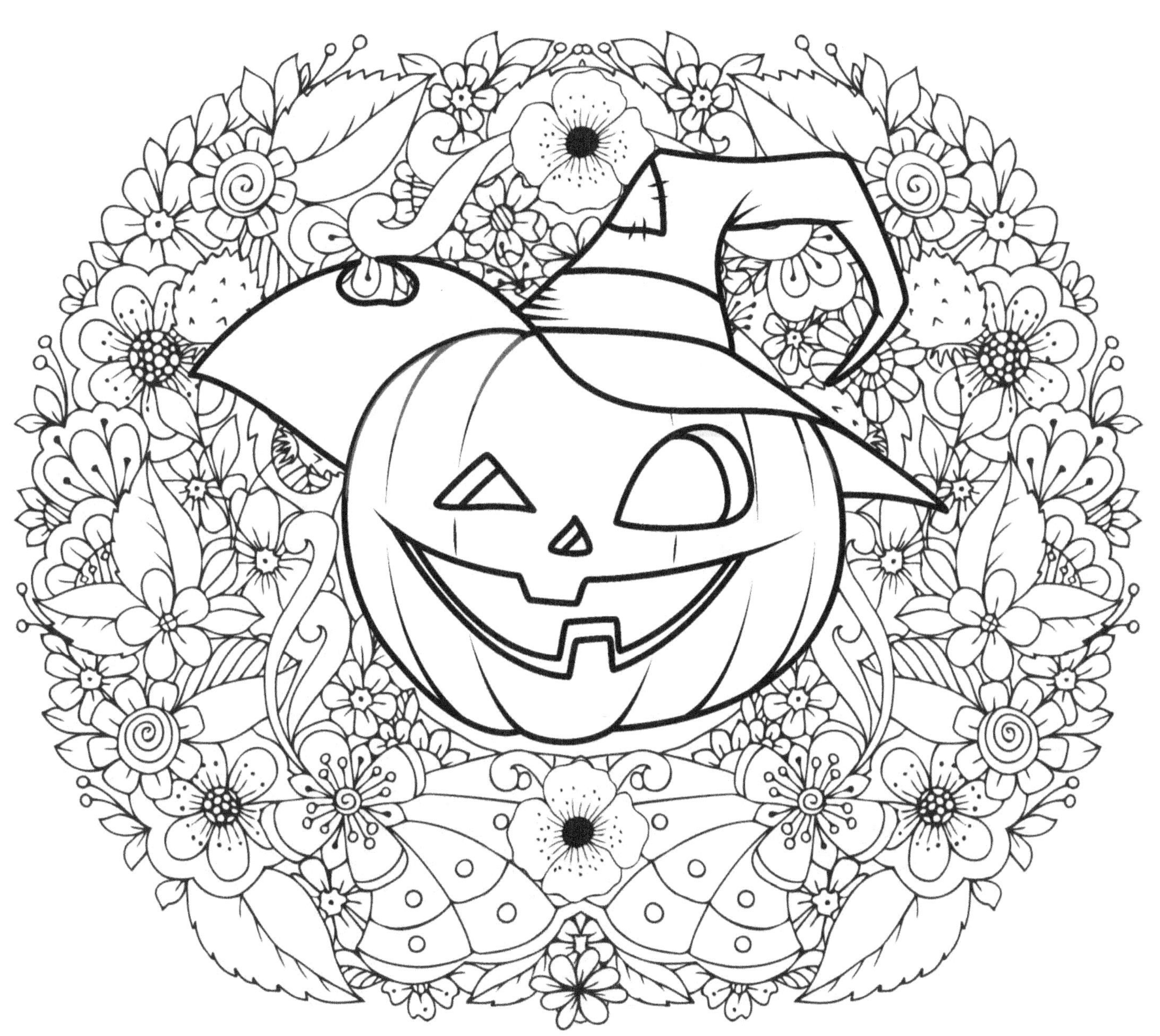

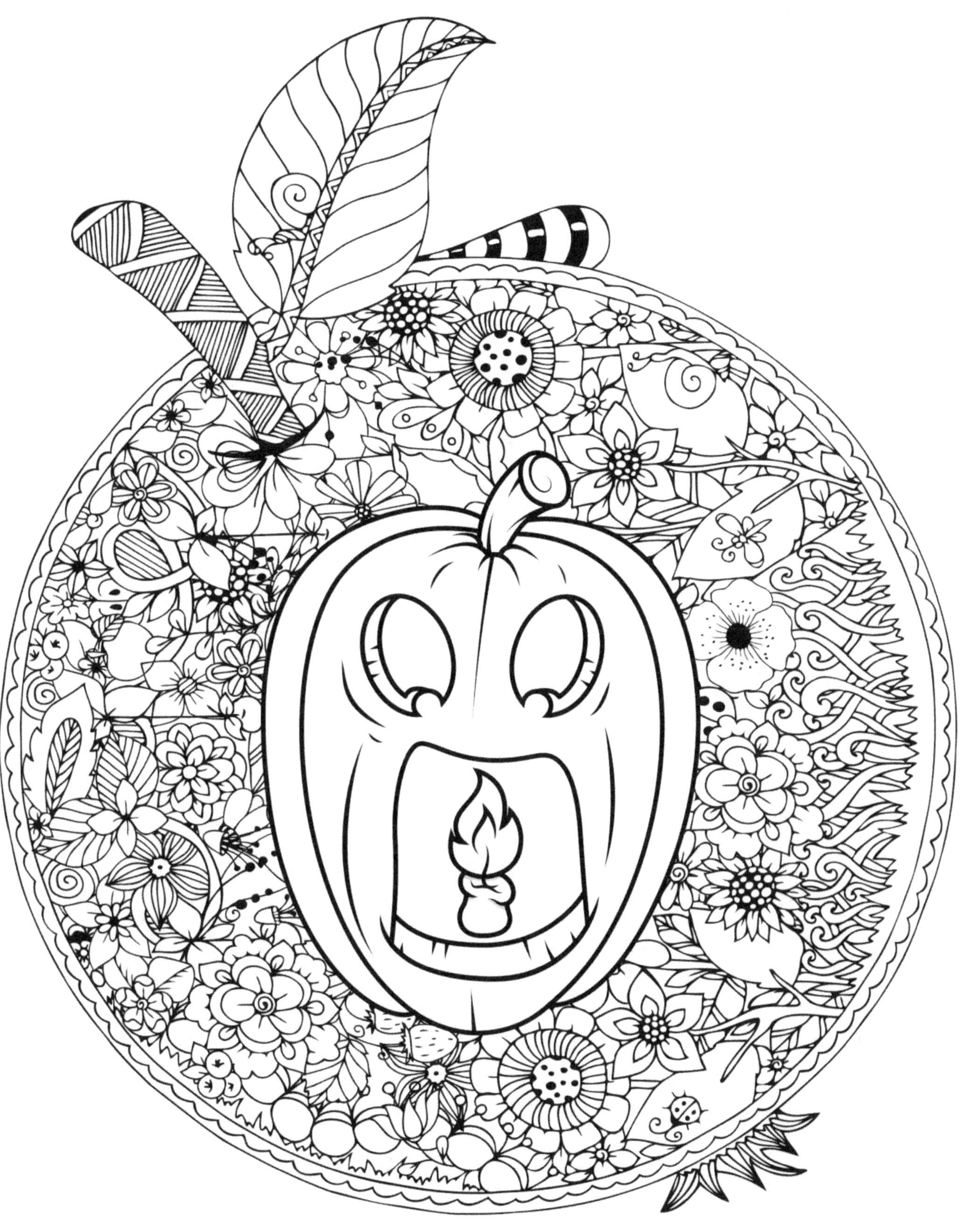

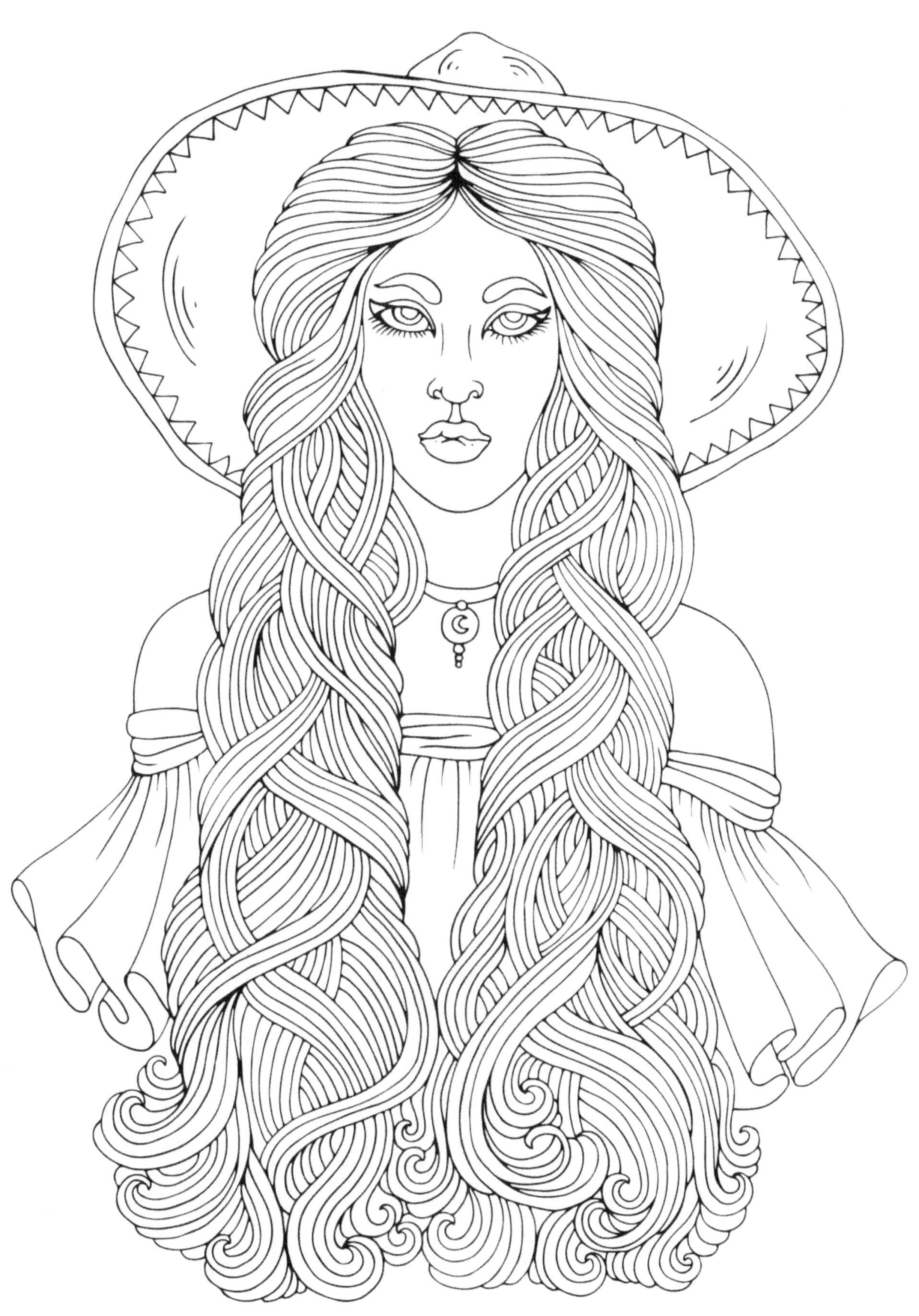

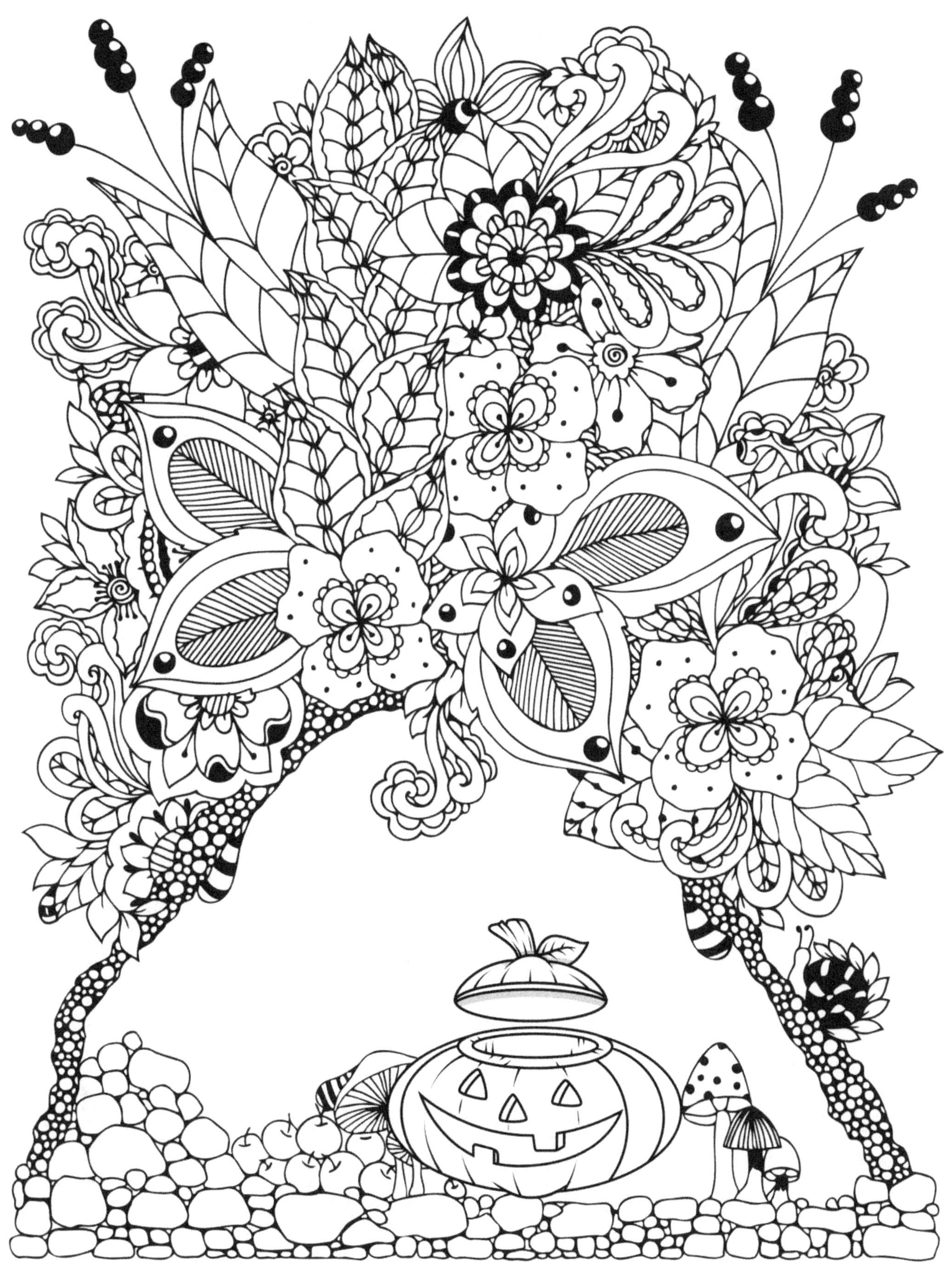

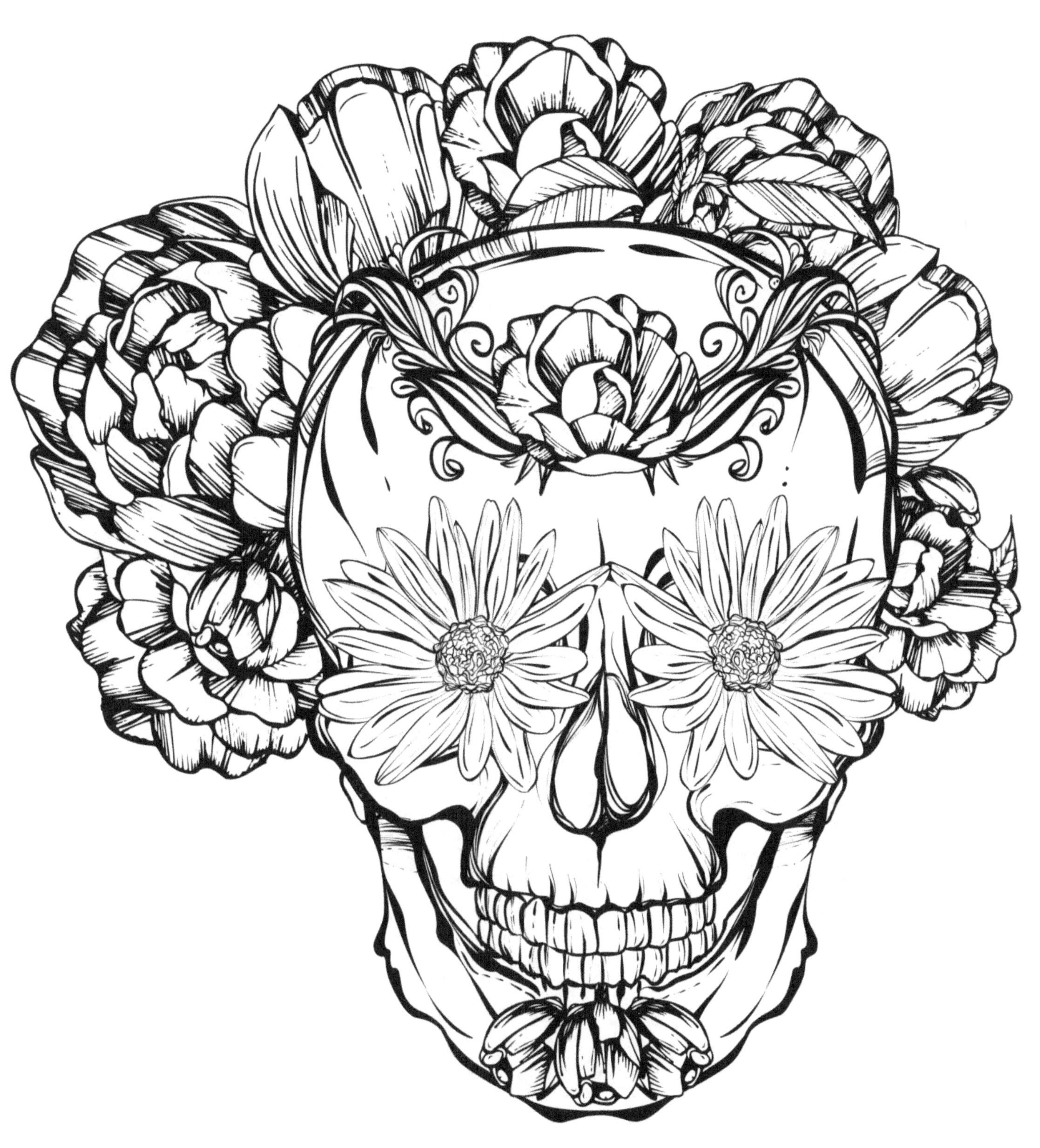

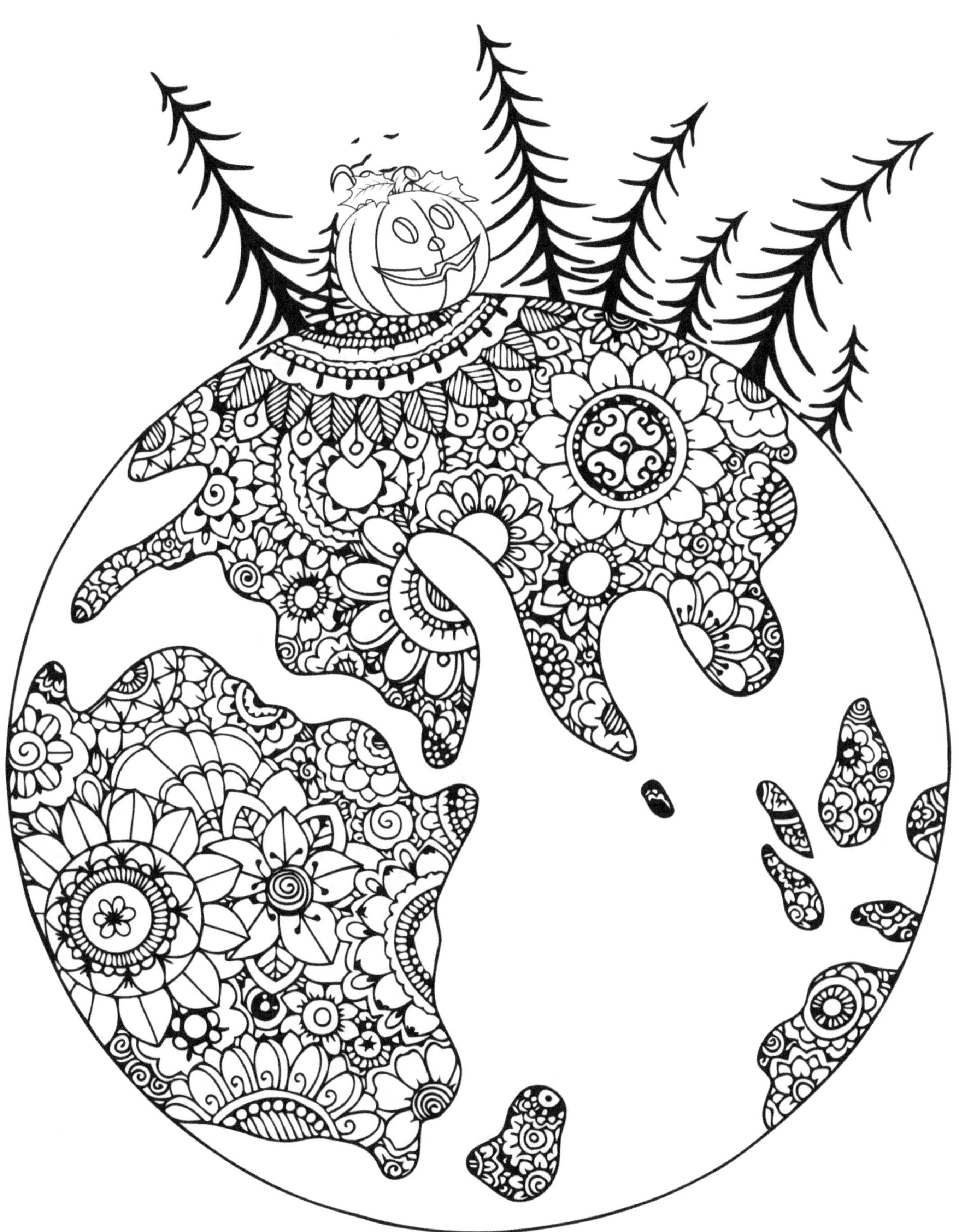

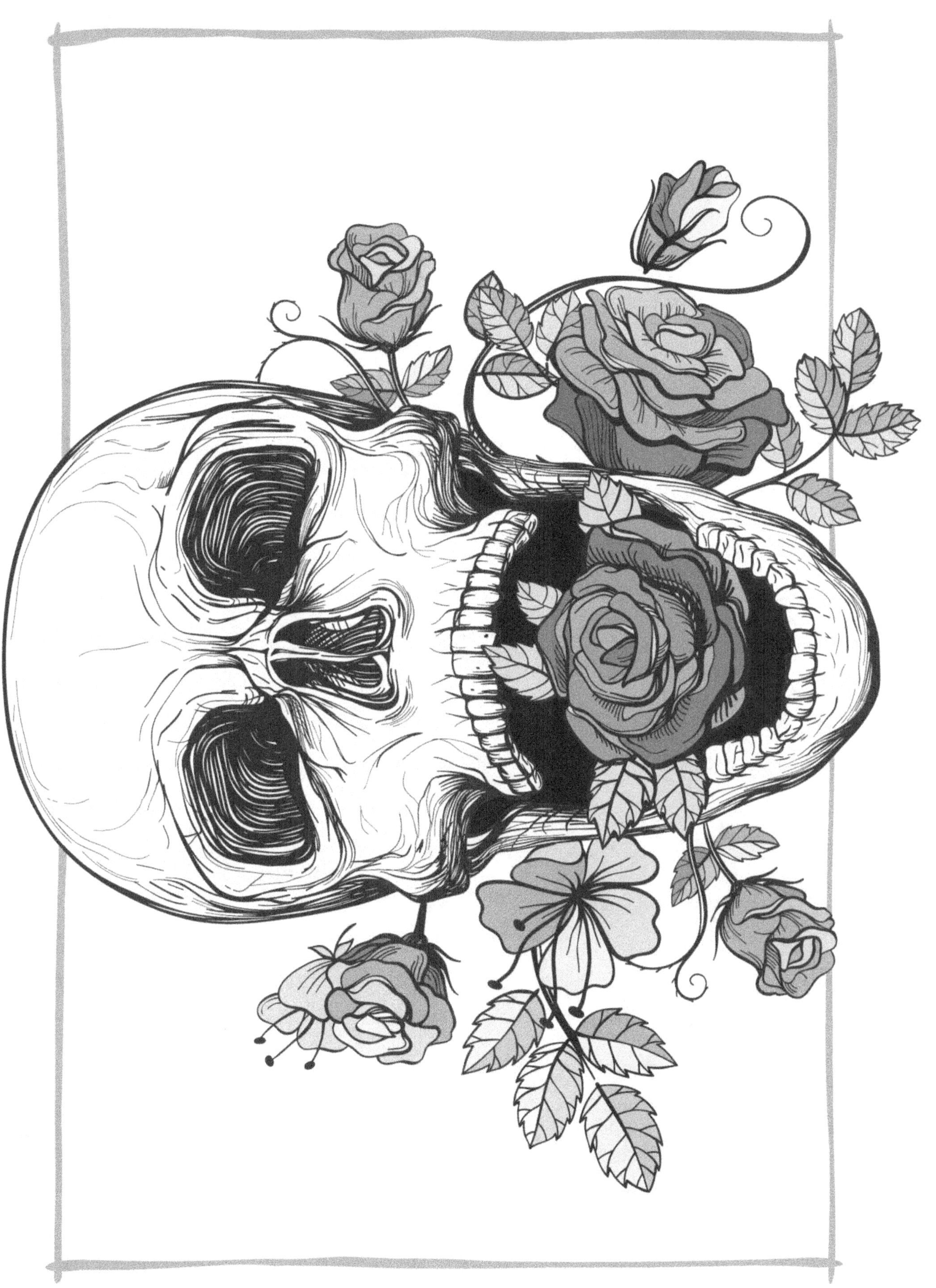

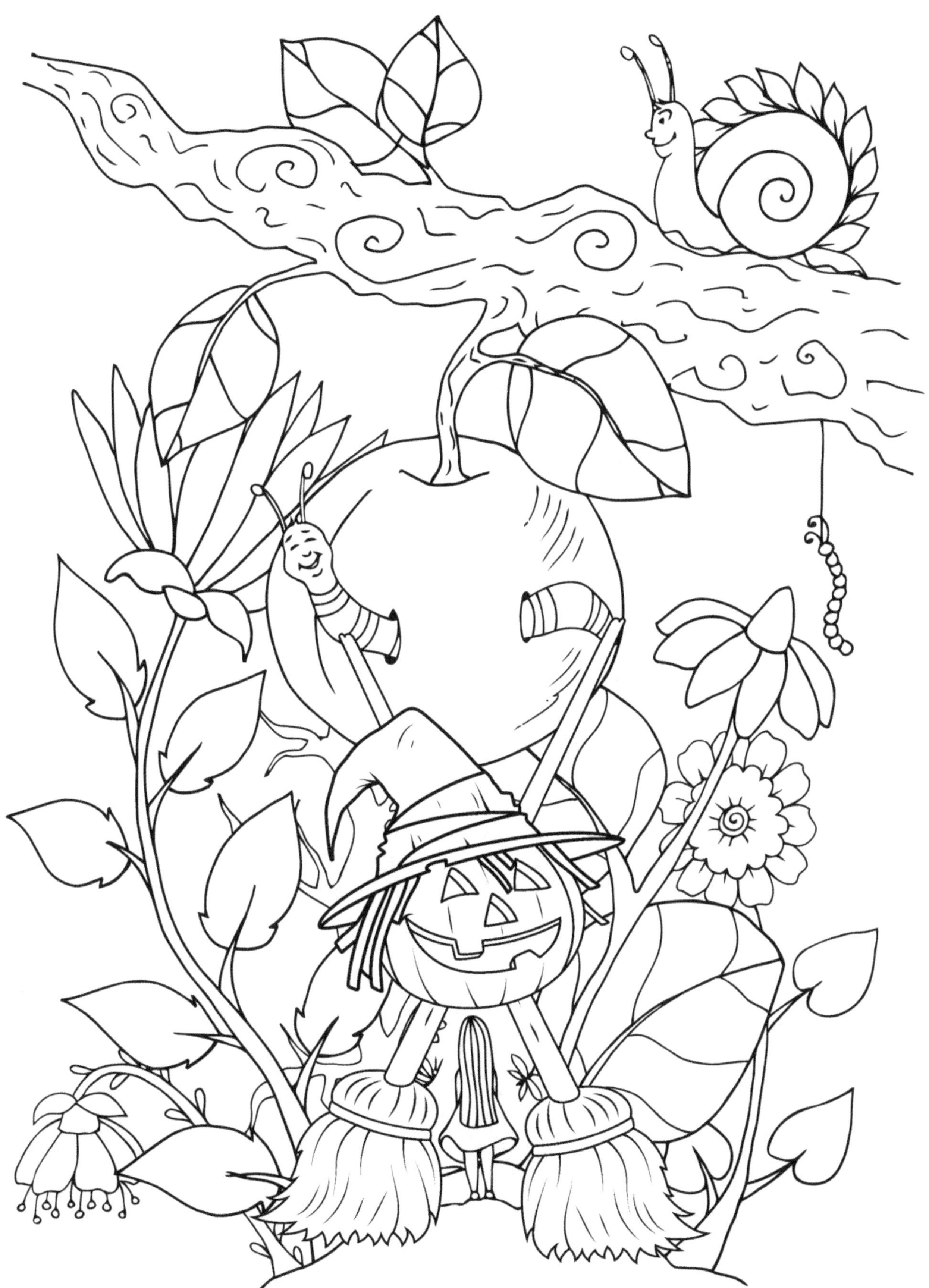

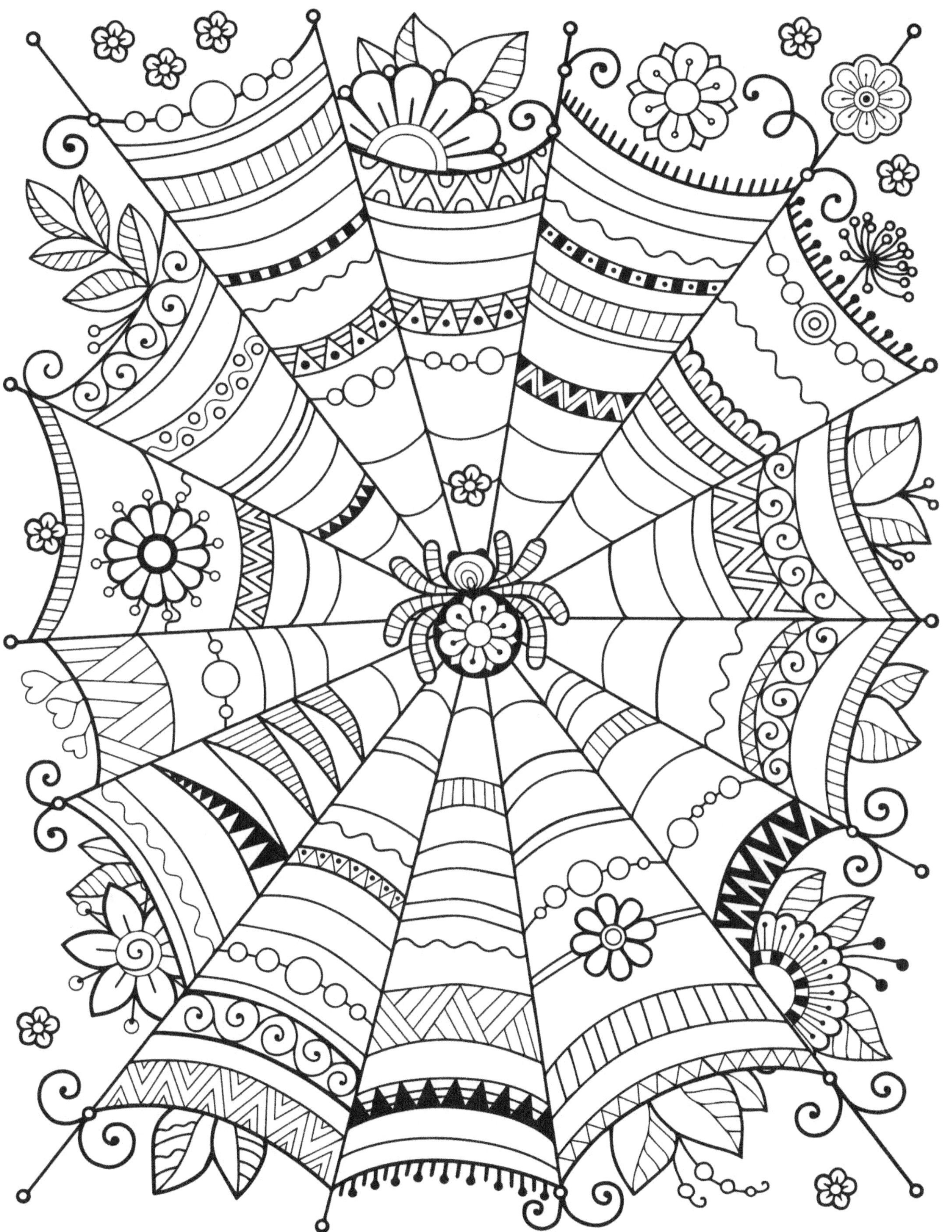

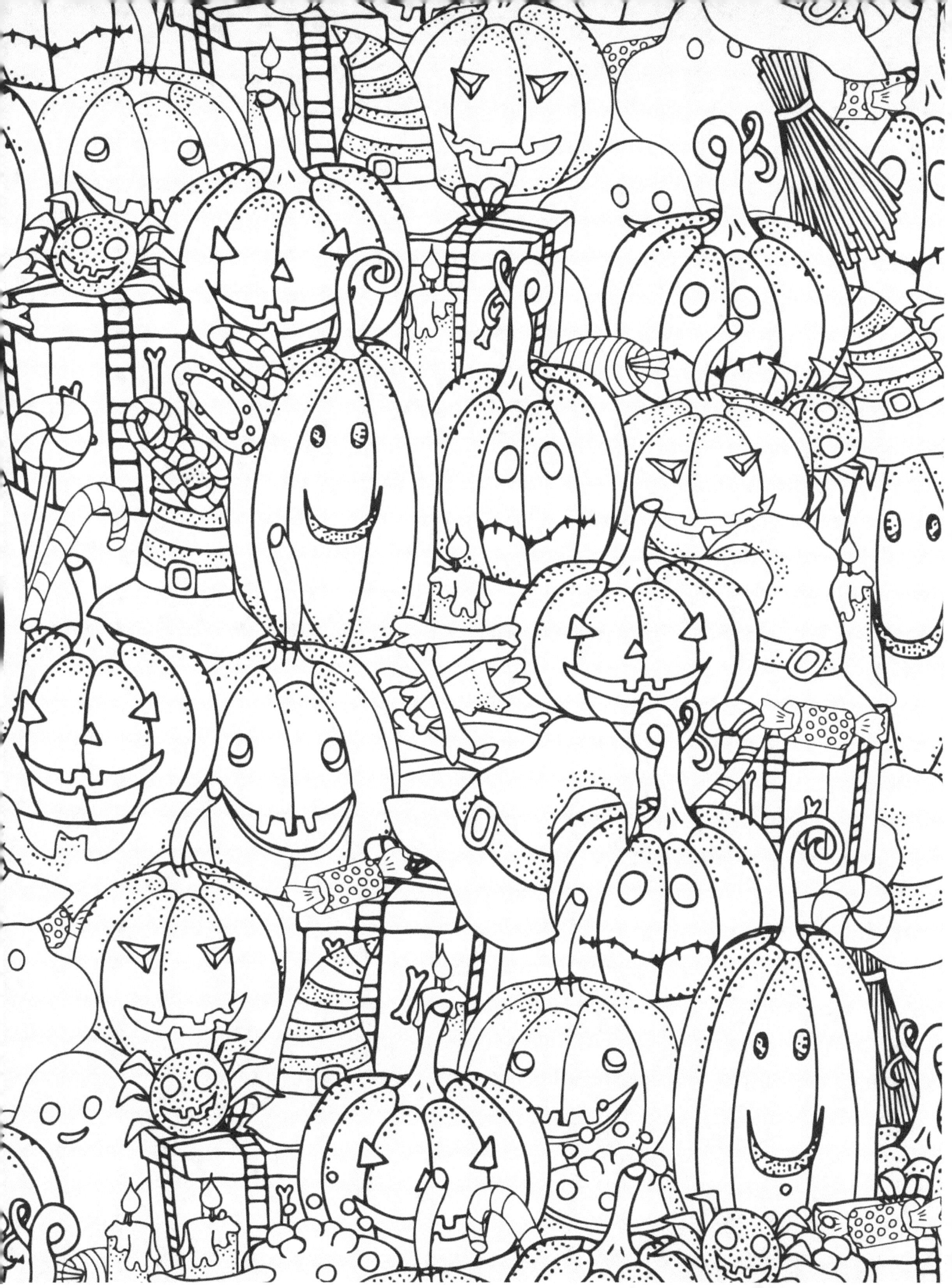

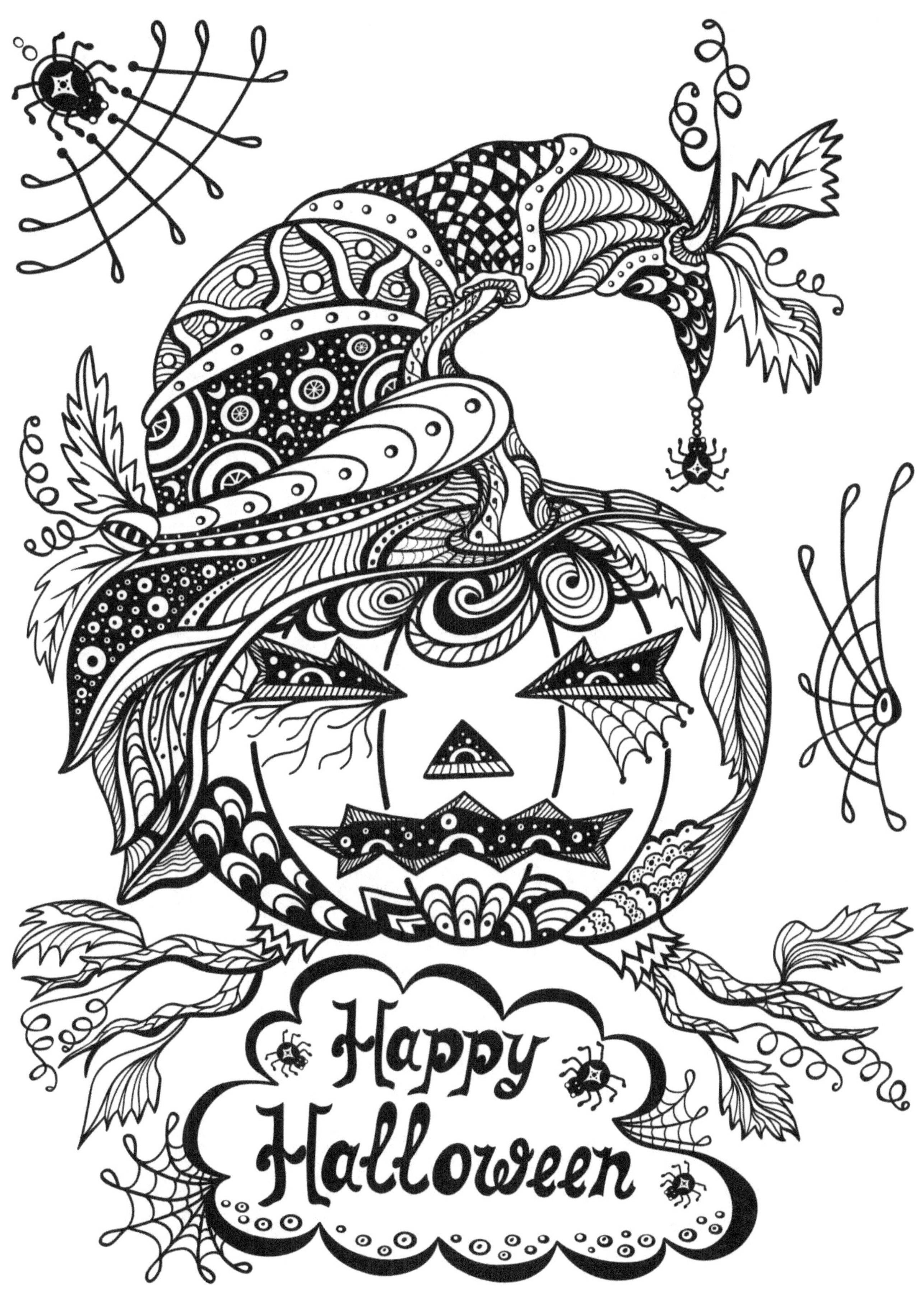

Happy
Halloween

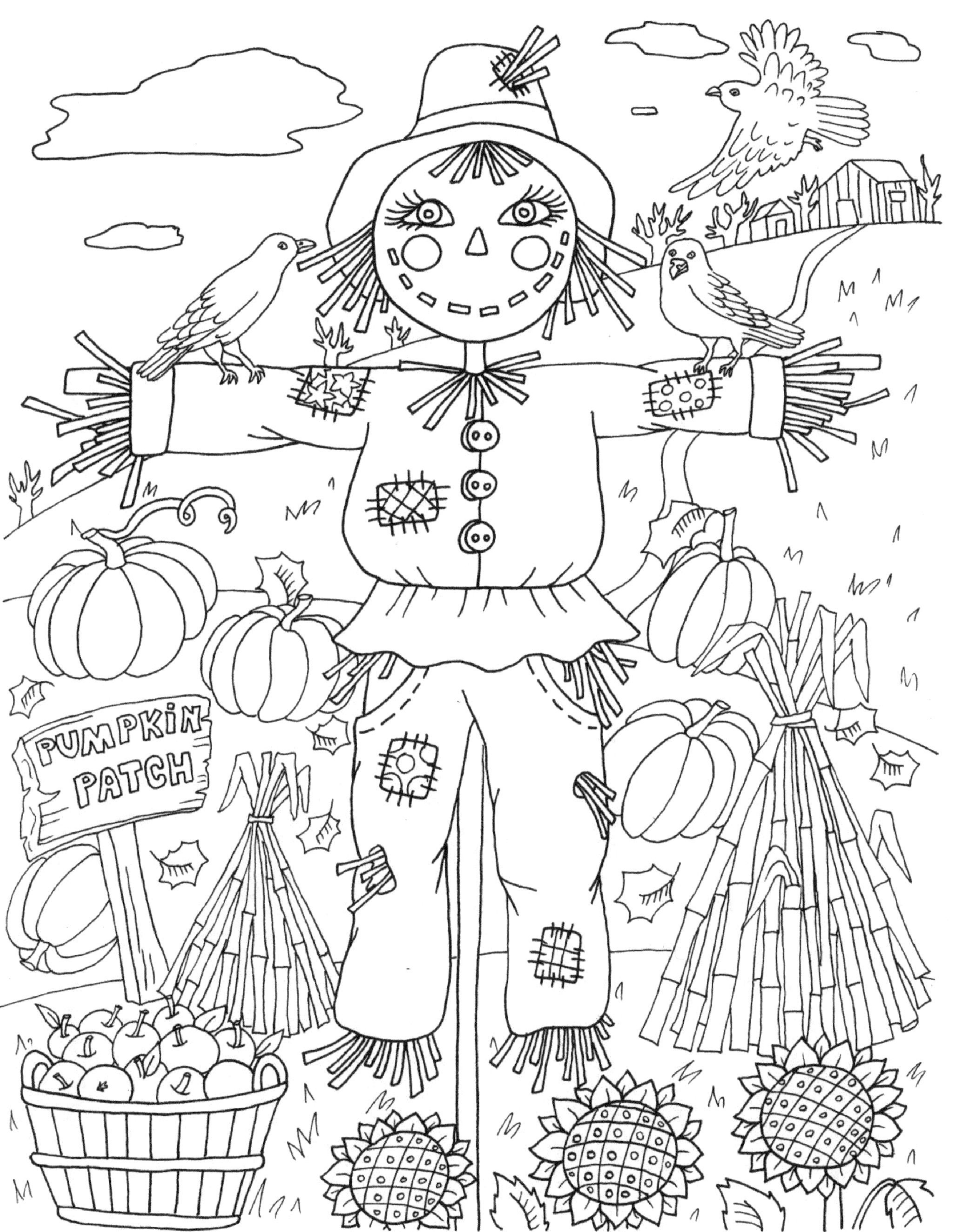
PUMPKIN PATCH

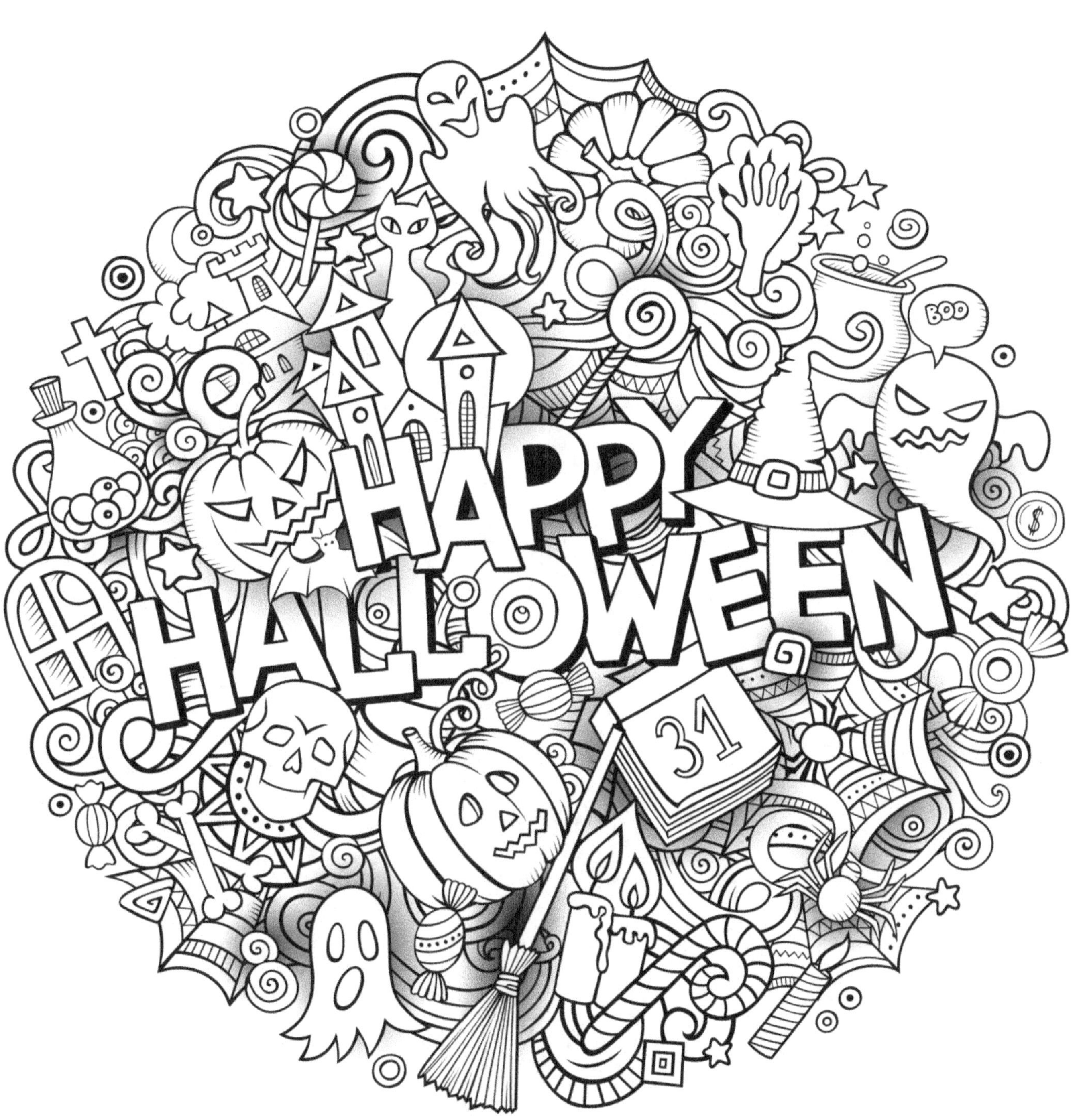

HAPPY
HALLOWEEN
BOO
31

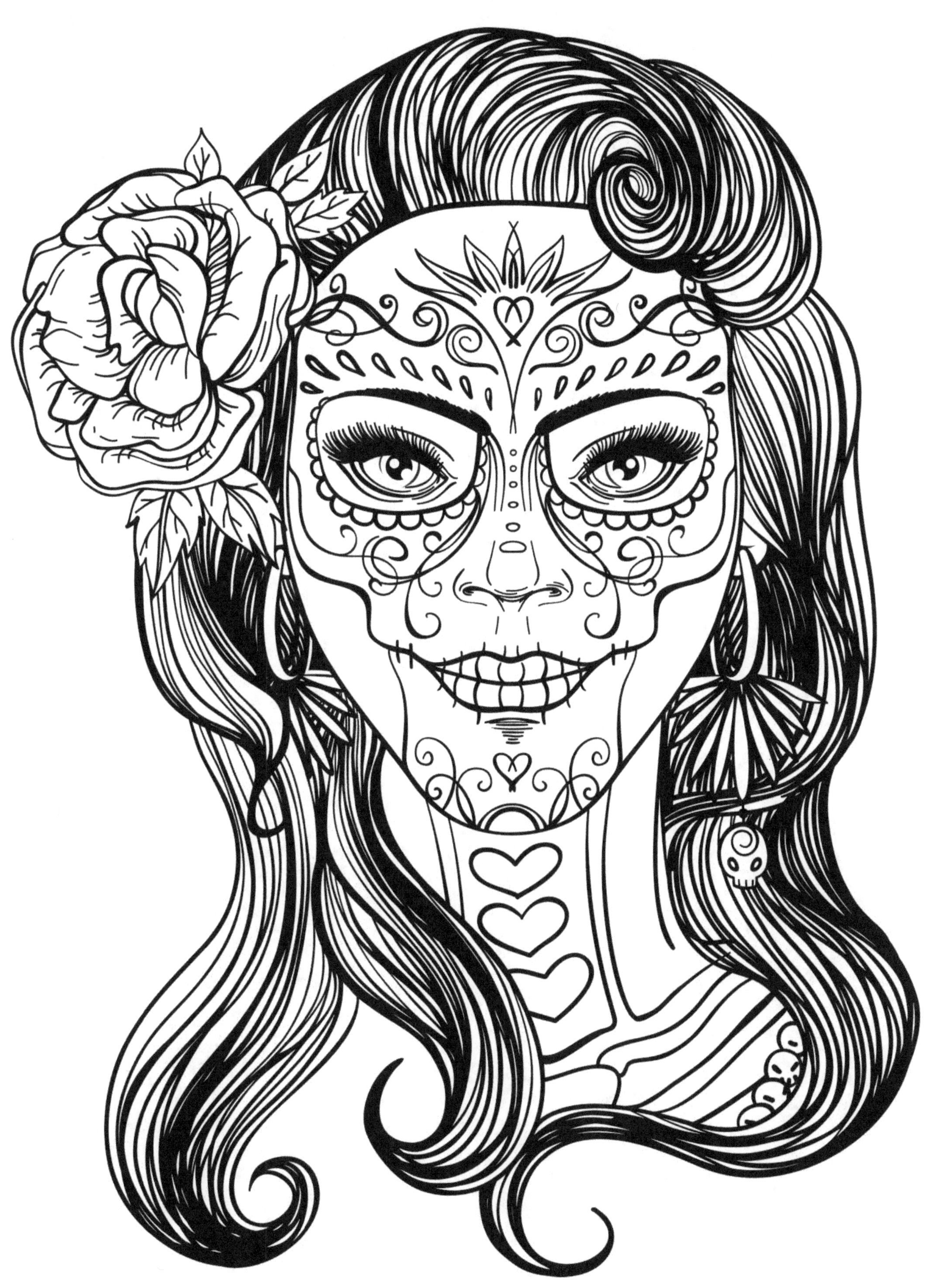